*The New*

**EXPLORERS**

# Animal Intelligence

## Why Is This Dolphin Smiling?

Produced in cooperation with

### WTTW Chicago

and

### Kurtis Productions, Ltd.

Adapted by
**Elaine Pascoe**

A BLACKBIRCH PRESS BOOK
WOODBRIDGE, CONNECTICUT

Published by Blackbirch Press, Inc.
260 Amity Road
Woodbridge, CT 06525

**web site:** http://www.blackbirch.com
**email:** staff@blackbirch.com

**For WTTW Chicago**
Edward Menaker, Executive Producer
**For Kurtis Productions, Ltd.**
Bill Kurtis, Executive Producer

Printed in the United States of America

10 9 8 7 6 5 4 3 2 1

**Library of Congress Cataloging-in-Publication Data**

Pascoe, Elaine.
    Animal intelligence : why is this dolphin smiling? / by Elaine Pascoe.
       p.   cm. — (New explorers)
    Includes bibliographical references and index.
    Summary: Examines dolphin intelligence and the ways in which dolphins communicate among themselves and with humans.
    ISBN 1-56711-226-9 (lib. bdg. : alk. paper)
    1. Dolphins—Juvenile literature. 2. Animal Intelligence—Juvenile literature. 3. Animal Communication—Juvenile literature. 4. Human–Animal Communication—Juvenile literature. [1. Dolphins. 2. Animal Intelligence. 3. Animal Communication. 4. Human-animal communication.] I. Title. II. Series.
QL737.C432P37   1998
599.5'3—dc20
                                    96-42983
                                    CIP
                                    AC

# INTRODUCTION

In 1990, I was lucky enough to help create a very special new "club." Its members come from all corners of the earth and are of all ages. They can be found braving crowded cities, floating among brilliantly colored coral reefs, and scaling desolate mountaintops. We call these people "New Explorers" because—in one way or another—they seek to uncover important knowledge or travel to places that others merely dream of.

No matter where they are, or what they do, New Explorers dedicate their lives to expanding the horizons of their science. Some are biologists. Others are physicists, neurosurgeons, or ethnobotanists. Still others are engineers, teachers, even cave divers. Each of them has worked hard to push limits—to go the extra step in the pursuit of a truly significant discovery.

In his quest for a breakthrough, Mike Madden is a typical New Explorer. For eight years, he was obsessed with proving that a 27-mile (44-kilometer) underwater cave system was actually connected to the Caribbean Sea. To do this, Madden swam through tunnels never before traveled by humans. Each dive was a calculated risk—a very great one—but well worth it, for Madden also proved this was the longest underwater cave system in the world.

Madden's story, like those of all the New Explorers, is what science is all about. Science is about adventure. It's about curiosity and discovery. And, sometimes, science is also about danger.

New Explorers make it clear that science is not confined to laboratories or classrooms. They show us that science is all around us; it's at the dark and frigid bottom of our oceans, it's inside an atom, it's light-years away in a galaxy we've yet to discover. My goal—and that of this series—is to travel along with people who are pursuing the seemingly impossible; journeying into the unknown. We want to be there as scientists and innovators make their discoveries. And we want you to be part of the process of discovery as well.

Accompanying these bold and courageous individuals—and documenting their work—has not been a simple task. When Mike Madden finally made his breakthrough, I—and the New Explorers camera crew—was there in the water with him. Over the years, I have also climbed into eagles' nests, tracked a deadly virus, cut my way through thick South American rain forests, trekked deep into East Africa's Masai territory, and flown jet fighters high above the clouds with some of the U.S. Air Force's most fearless Top Guns.

As you witness the achievements we bring you through New Explorers books, you may start thinking that most of the world's great discoveries have already been made, that all the great frontiers have already been explored. But nothing could be further from the truth. In fact, scientists and researchers are now uncovering more uncharted frontiers than ever before.

As host and executive producer of our television program, my mission is to find the most fascinating and exciting New Explorers of our time. I hope that their adventures will inspire you to undertake adventures of your own—to seek out and be curious, to find answers and contemplate or create solutions. At the very best, these stories will turn you into one of the world's Newest Explorers—the men and women who will capture our imaginations and thrill us with discoveries well into the 21st century.

*Bill Kurtis*

Bill Kurtis

The New
EXPLORERS

On cue, the dolphins leap out of the water, arc through the air, and dive. They are polished performers, and the audience loves their show. But these dolphins are much more. They are the focus of exciting new research into questions that have puzzled people for centuries.

**H**ello, I'm Bill Kurtis. It's no wonder we've always been fascinated by dolphins. Our affection for these animals has been reflected in stories and art through the ages, from ancient Greek myths to television shows and motion pictures.

People have a special bond with dolphins. These creatures seem to like us, and they seem to have much in common with us. They even seem to smile. And in our fondness for dolphins, we tend to humanize them—that is, we suppose that they have human qualities. In fact, we've so humanized these animals that some people wouldn't be at all surprised to see one walk out of the ocean and recite Shakespeare.

And so we wonder: Are dolphins intelligent? If we listened carefully enough, learned their language, could they talk to us? And more important, could we learn to communicate with them, these creatures from another world?

The idea of communicating with another species is intriguing. And the idea of communicating with the dolphin is especially so. Some scientists believe the size of the dolphin's brain alone indicates higher intelligence—it's at least three times larger than a house cat's. At three and a half pounds, it's a half pound larger than the human brain.

But can dolphins reason, and how can we find out? In this edition of the NEW EXPLORERS, we'll observe the work of scientists who are seeking answers to questions such as these—scientists like Chicago's Randy Brill.

Randy Brill's efforts have taken him where no one else has had the patience to go.

Sensory psychologist Randy Brill headed a dolphin study based at Chicago's Brookfield Zoo.

Randy Brill is on the cutting edge of dolphin research. And he is uniquely qualified to explore the question of how dolphins communicate. A doctor in sensory psychology, Randy has worked with these animals as supervisor of marine mammal training at Brookfield Zoo, outside Chicago. There, the dolphins at the Seven Seas Panorama—Angie, Nemo, Shana, Windy, and Stormy—put on shows for the public. They're also at the heart of some ground-breaking studies.

Randy Brill's efforts have taken him where no one else has had the patience to go; into an experiment to learn how the dolphin hears. His focus is not on conventional sounds, the sounds that we hear above water. Instead, it's on the high-pitched sounds that dolphins use underwater. These sounds allow dolphins to signal great distances and to navigate in darkness with the amazing system known as echolocation. Echolocation may even allow dolphins to see in a third dimension, penetrating objects to "read" them like an electronic ray gun.

# ECHOLOCATION

Echolocation is like sonar. The dolphin fires a burst of sound from its head and receives it back. This allows it to judge distances and identify objects. You can see a dolphin's head move from side to side as it scans an object with its beam of sound. And if you're in the water, you can almost feel the echolocation signals. One researcher described the feeling as "a dotted line going through your body."

This zipping or buzzing sound—really a stream of high-pitched clicks—is very different from the sounds a dolphin makes in the open air. The underwater sound beam strikes objects and bounces back, reflecting not just surfaces but also air spaces inside, such as a swimmer's lungs. It scans an object in much the same way that ultrasound imaging allows doctors to see inside the human body. It also helps dolphins to communicate underwater, allowing them to signal great distances when they find food or are in danger.

## Echolocation in Dolphins

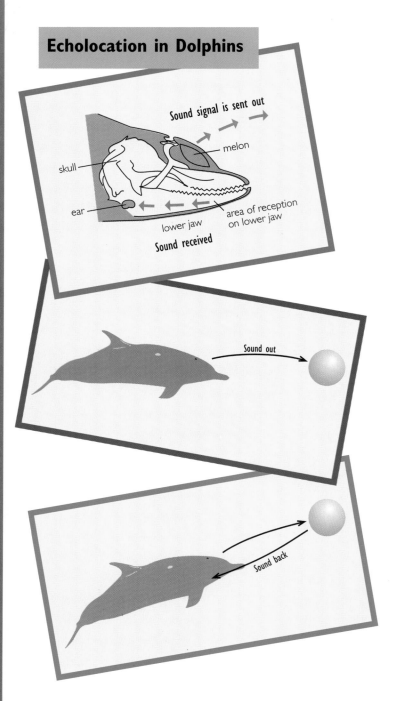

Randy says, "There's been a theory for years that the dolphin sends sounds out of an area of its forehead called the melon, and receives the sound back not in its ears, on the side of its head, but in its lower jaw. It's a very difficult theory to prove because, to find out, the trainer has to ask the animal to go temporarily blind and deaf—and that's the kind of trust that is almost impossible to ask for."

While many scientists were asking questions about dolphin intelligence, Randy Brill and his dedicated staff at Brookfield Zoo were pursuing basic science through their experiment. They went through months of agonizing and tedious repetitions, not knowing if they would succeed. But they were confident that if they could learn more about the dolphin's remarkable sound machine, it would help in another important quest—one that could eventually lead toward real communication with these animals.

That's a goal people have been hoping to achieve since ancient times.

## THE DOLPHIN CONNECTION TO PEOPLE

From the time of the ancient Greeks to the mid-twentieth century, our knowledge of dolphins came from observation in the open sea. Stories of dolphins befriending children and lost swimmers have been recorded in every part of the world. They were the kind of stories that painted a warm picture of a marine friend for humans. But the picture wasn't quite as pleasant for the dolphin. Its worst enemies turned out to be humans.

Thousands of dolphins are killed in tuna nets from which they can't escape. These nets violate marine-mammal protection laws, but they are still used. Marine biologists have asked governments to strengthen and enforce the laws. Dolphins aren't endangered yet, but protecting them requires constant vigilance. Their safest homes are often those created for them by humans.

**Left:** Humans have long had a special affection for dolphins. Because of their unusual intelligence, dolphins have also prompted a great deal of human study.

Dolphin shows, like this one at San Diego's Sea World, are always among the most popular.

In the mid-1950s, the first marine studios opened to the public. The original idea behind them was that the dolphins would entertain the public by putting on shows, and the price of admission would support basic animal research. In many cases, however, there was far more entertainment going on than research. But scientists were able to observe dolphins up close for the first time. This helped to kick dolphin research into high gear.

One of the first things scientists noticed was the willingness of dolphins to imitate the human voice above water. At the same time, other scientists became intrigued with the dolphin's large, complex brain. They reasoned that, since dolphins have been around for 60 million years—millions of years longer than humans—dolphins must be capable of the same kinds of computations as humans. That is, dolphins and humans might have similar mental abilities.

Dolphin researcher, John Lilly.

Lilly created a language in which a computer translates human words into dolphin sounds.

Still another scientist, Dr. John Lilly, put those two observations together. He wondered if dolphins were trying to communicate with humans—even to the point of matching our voices, our laughter, and other noises played for them in the laboratory.

Lilly personally raised the money that was needed to build the Communications Research Institute on St. Thomas, in the Virgin Islands. There, he tried to prove his theory. He created a language in which a computer translated human words like "fish" into dolphin sounds. The dolphin could not only hear the translated word, but could also see it on an underwater television screen.

In Lilly's experiments, dolphins responded to words and seemed to match the sounds made by people with underwater sounds of their own. One of his observers, Margaret Howe, also tried to teach a dolphin to make the sounds of English speech in the open air, in a way that people could understand. Again, the dolphin seemed to respond and answer.

Was it a breakthrough in communication with another species? Or was it just another of the many examples of animals mimicking humans? Whichever it was, the exciting moment was immortalized in a film, *Day of the Dolphin*, starring George C. Scott. The film was fiction, but it was based on Lilly's work. The movie was made despite Lilly's objections. He was most concerned that the film gave audiences the impression that dolphins could talk.

Many of Lilly's colleagues felt that he got carried away with his theory. They were left to answer the questions it raised: Are dolphins really that intelligent? If they could just unlock our language, could they introduce us to a whole new world?

A lot of scientists think we're asking the wrong questions about dolphins. We tend to judge them by how much they reflect our culture. Far more exciting, these scientists argue, is how dolphins have survived for 60 million years in their own world.

At Lilly's research center, a computer translated human words into dolphin sounds.

# Dolphin Data

The dolphins we see performing at ocean parks are bottlenose dolphins, one of several kinds of dolphins that are found worldwide. They are famous for their friendliness and curiosity toward people, and they do well in captivity. Here are some facts about them.

• Like all dolphins, the bottlenose is a mammal—it must come to the surface to breathe. It inhales and exhales quickly through a blowhole at the top of its head, and then dives again. It usually surfaces this way several times a minute, but it can hold its breath up to ten minutes.

• Most full-grown bottlenose dolphins are 8 or 9 feet (3 meters) long. But some are up to 12 feet (4 meters) long and weigh more than 400 pounds (182 kilograms).

• The bottlenose swims mainly with its powerful, streamlined tail. As the tail moves up and down, the flukes (fins) at

A group of performing bottlenose dolphins

the end drive the dolphin forward.

• Like other mammals, dolphins bear live young. The female bottlenose carries a single calf for about 12 months. It is born in the water, tail first, and she immediately helps it to the surface, so that it can breathe.

A bottlenose family with young

• A bottlenose calf swims alongside its mother, with one fin touching the mother's side. Like all mammals, it drinks its mother's milk. Her milk glands have special muscles that squirt milk into the calf's mouth.

Dolphins breathe through a blowhole.

• Dolphins don't sleep for hours at a time, the way other mammals do. Instead, they take brief naps throughout the day. They can even nap while they swim.

• The bottlenose has about 90 teeth. It uses them for catching fish and squid—but not for chewing. Instead, the bottlenose prefers to eat its fish whole, usually taking it in head first.

# BOLD NEW QUESTIONS

Dr. Ken Norris, who directs dolphin studies for the University of California at Santa Cruz, works with these animals at the edge of Monterey Bay. Says Norris, "I don't think there's any question that dolphins are high-level mammals, or that they're conscious, or that they think. Those things are givens as far as I'm concerned."

In intelligence, Norris ranks dolphins somewhere on the level of the primates (monkeys, apes, and humans). But, he notes, they are very different—especially in their amazing ability to use sound:

"I think they're among the world's most remarkable acoustic animals. They can process sound ten times as fast as we can, and they can hear sounds ten times as high. And they use these abilities throughout their lives."

But, Norris adds, "I don't see any evidence at all that they have a language like a human language."

"They are among the world's most remarkable acoustic animals."

Dr. Ken Norris

# BRAIN SIZE AND BRAIN POWER

Could dolphins be as intelligent as people? Some researchers have turned to the size of the dolphin brain for clues. Here's how a dolphin's brain compares with a human brain and that of a chimpanzee, another animal known for intelligence:

**Dolphin:**
Brain weight: 3.5 pounds (1.6 kilograms)
Body weight: 300 pounds (136 kilograms)
Brain as a percent of body weight: 1.19%
**Human:**
Brain weight: 3.1 pounds (1.4 kilograms)
Body weight: 150 pounds (68 kilograms)
Brain as a percent of body weight: 2.1%
**Chimpanzee:**
Brain weight: 0.75 pound (.34 kilogram)
Body weight: 110 pounds (49.9 kilograms)
Brain as a percent of body weight: 0.70%

If brain size is linked to brain power, then dolphins would be considered to be more advanced then chimpanzees. The catch is that brain size alone isn't necessarily a reliable sign of intelligence. Nor is the size of brain structures such as the cerebral cortex—the "gray matter" that is responsible for the complex functions of learning, memory, creativity, and other higher brain activities. Some animals, such as the spiny anteater, have a very large amount of gray matter relative to their body size, but they're still not considered to be even above average in intelligence. Only further scientific research—done with all kinds of animals—will help to resolve some of the questions that remain about intelligence and brain size.

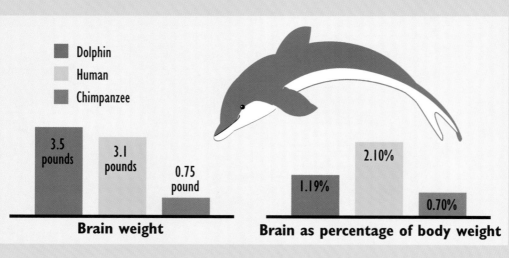

What makes human language so effective is syntax—arranging words into phrases and sentences that communicate facts, emotions, even abstract thought. There is no evidence that dolphins have anything like syntax. And that is one reason Norris started searching for answers in another direction. He is probing the behavior of the dolphin—and what may be a far more efficient method of communication in the open sea.

That's where Randy Brill's experiment enters the picture. Establishing once and for all how a dolphin hears high-pitched underwater sounds takes us one step closer to understanding what dolphins are saying. But theory is much easier to come by than fact.

## SLOW PROGRESS

The idea behind Randy Brill's experiment was to have a dolphin named Nemo tell the difference between two objects—a metal cylinder and a sand-filled ring—using only his echolocation. An object would be placed in the water ahead of him. If he identified it as the cylinder, he would wheel back to the edge of the pool and hit a float. If he identified the ring, he would remain in place.

To make sure that Nemo used only his echolocation, the researchers would cover his eyes with eye cups. To learn if he actually received his echolocation signals in his lower jaw, they would try to cover his jaw with a sort of hood. If Nemo could identify the cylinder and ring with the eye cups on, but not when the hood covered his jaw, Randy would know for sure that Nemo received signals through his jaw.

The experiment progressed slowly. At first, the researchers had a hard time getting Nemo to pick out the two objects. Randy explains, "He's used to going out in the show blindfolded and telling the difference between two objects. But for some reason, he wasn't getting the concept in this context. Then, added to that, were the problems we were having introducing the hood—he kept shaking it off. I would wake up in the morning with what pregnant women would recognize as morning sickness, just wondering, 'Am I going to make it today?'"

"Any trainer will admit that, especially when it comes to dolphins, it's a question of who trains whom. Lots of times I leave at night imagining that the dolphins are having a conversation—that they're saying, 'Yeah, you should have seen what I got the big, bearded guy to do today.'

"I don't think anyone can work with the kinds of animals we work with and not walk away feeling that you're watching decision making in action, that there's some purpose behind a lot of the things the animals do. In my work, it's obvious that we've just scratched the surface. Compared to what there is to learn about the dolphin, we're just at the beginning. And who knows what we're going to uncover."

# CAN ANIMALS USE LANGUAGE?

Until recently, we've always distinguished the human brain by its ability to link new information to memory, to produce new ideas and imagination. Animals also have memory, but scientists have thought that animal memories are limited to direct associations. Nemo does a trick because he knows he'll get a reward. That is, he associates the trick with rewards he's received in the past. But some recent studies are making scientists reconsider the way animals use memory.

An example is Alex, an African gray parrot. Chosen at random from a pet store, Alex was trained intensively by Irene Pepperburg at Northwestern

Irene Pepperburg

Alex the parrot

University. When Irene gives Alex an object—a stone or a stick—he responds with the English word for it. He can also identify quantities of objects, up to and including six.

Is Alex just imitating sounds, or is he actually using a language?

Irene says, "I hesitate to call it language. But what he is doing is using the sounds of English speech to communicate with us. It's more than simple mimicry because he responds to the particular objects themselves and to the particular questions that we ask."

This is significant because birds have a different type of brain than mammals do. Higher mammals use a part of the brain called the cerebral neocortex for most of their thinking. In a bird's brain, there isn't much cerebral neocortex.

Alex can distinguish the subtle differences between similar objects.

Yet Alex is making judgments based on his memory and comprehension.

Alex is even able to distinguish similarities and differences between objects. In one test, for example, his trainer gives him two plastic keys, identical except for their color, and asks him, "What's different?" He responds clearly, "Color."

"This is a very important task," says Irene Pepperburg. "It involves the abstract concepts of same and different." The parrot is able to tell his trainer not just that the keys are different, but how they are different—in color. That is, he can label the quality that makes them different. "That's important because it means that we can show him two objects he's never seen before and ask him what is the same or different about them," says Irene.

In other words, the parrot seems to be able to apply his knowledge to new situations—in much the same way that people call on their memory stores to help in a new situation. If a parrot can do this, what can a dolphin do—with a cerebral neocortex even larger than ours?

"It's just amazing what dolphins can do with their echolocation ability"

Researchers know that dolphin echolocation is a highly complex and evolved process.

The researchers kept at it, eager to learn the secrets of the dolphin's incredibly sophisticated echolocation system. "It's just amazing what dolphins can do with their echolocation ability," says Randy. "We humans have been unable to mechanically reproduce it, and there may well be benefits if we could unlock the secrets— what information do you use, and how do you use it? What is it that tells you that two objects are of different sizes or densities?

"There's been talk in the past about developing echolocation-type devices that blind folks could use. A sound generator, mounted on glasses or some kind of carrier, would produce a signal that people could hear, and a person could be trained to listen to the returning echo and gain information about what's out in front. If we can understand what's important in echolocation signals, what carries the information that's necessary, we'll come a step closer to using it for our benefit. And we'll answer a lot of questions about the dolphin."

Outside the dolphin arena, September turned into spring. Randy and his staff were trying to be patient with their experiment. They filled their days giving shows and traveling to the Parmley Hearing Institute, at Loyola University, to analyze Nemo's echolocation signals on a computer.

The clicks that make up the echolocation signals are so fast that only a computer can really follow them. But the dolphin's mental computations must be equally fast. That raises a question. If the dolphin's echolocation creates images in three dimensions, like holographs, could dolphins be communicating with each other by using holographic pictures as their language, the way humans use words?

Randy Brill has spent endless days in the water studying dolphin behavior.

Bill Kurtis and Randy Brill watch a computer monitor displaying echolocation signals.

The answer to that question comes from Hawaii, at Kewalo Basin Laboratory. There, trainers under the direction of Lou Herman have taught dolphins to understand the meaning, not only of words, but of sentences. In fact, the Kewalo Basin dolphins understand a thousand sentences, based on a 50-to-60 word vocabulary. The trainers communicate the sentences by hand gestures and by computer signals that are broadcast into the dolphins' tank.

"In our program, we work with animals over a period of years, in an intensive educational experience. And we can begin to see what these animals are capable of. We have been, I think, the first project to demonstrate convincingly that any animal can really understand both the meanings of symbols and how different combinations of symbols can change meaning."

# DOLPHINS IN DANGER

Dolphins have few natural enemies. Killer whales (members of the dolphin family called orcas) and sharks are just about the only ocean animals that attack dolphins. But dolphins face danger from another source: humans.

Commercial tuna fishing poses the biggest threat. Schools of dolphins often swim above schools of tuna. Commercial fishing boats set out big nets to trap the tuna, and they trap the dolphins as well. Dolphins die when they are caught in nets—they can't get to the surface to breathe. By some estimates, hundreds of thousands have died this way.

In 1972, the United States enacted a law, the Marine Mammal Protection Act, which was aimed at ending this threat to dolphins. The law set limits on the number of dolphins U.S. tuna boats could kill. The U.S. fishing industry then switched to new nets, with special gateways that allowed dolphins (but not tuna) to escape.

"Safe" tuna logo

But thousands of dolphins still die in tuna nets—because boats from other countries don't always use the new nets. The United States has tried to ban imported tuna that is caught in old-style nets, but the ban has proved hard to enforce.

Many scientists and environmentalists are urging governments to do more. They also want people to know more about the dolphin. Learning about this remarkable animal, and appreciating what it can do, is the best hope for saving it.

A Pacific white-sided dolphin, caught in a tuna net.

To test the dolphins' skills, the trainers put a number of objects into the tank: a basket, a surfboard, a Frisbee, and a floating swimmer. The dolphins must distinguish between them—and the words, or signals, that stand for the objects—to carry out the trainers' commands. The trainers who give the signals wear eye goggles that keep them from seeing what the dolphins are doing. That way, they won't give the animals unconscious cues.

First, an easy one: The trainer signals the command "basket Frisbee in," telling the dolphin to put the Frisbee into the basket. The dolphin responds correctly at once.

A dolphin responds to a series of commands at Kewalo Basin.

Person Over

Then a harder command. The trainer signals "surfboard person fetch," telling the dolphin to take the person in the tank over to the surfboard. Again, the dolphin responds, pushing the floating swimmer to the board.

Finally, the sentence is changed just slightly—but enough to change its meaning. The trainer signals "person surfboard fetch," telling the dolphin to take the surfboard to the person. The dolphin understands completely.

Lou Herman doesn't pretend to be unlocking a language of dolphins. "Our program is deliberately aimed at the opposite," says Herman—at showing the dolphin's capacity to learn, by enriching its education.

"For five seconds, Nemo was blind and deaf."

## A Breakthrough and a Beginning

At Brookfield Zoo, nearly a year and a half after he began, Randy Brill arrived one morning for another training session with Nemo. This one, however, would be different from any other.

"One eye cup was on, the hood was put on, and then the second eye cup was put in place," he recalls. "For five seconds, Nemo was blind and deaf, and we all just let out a yelp like you wouldn't believe. Then things really started to roll." Nemo had finally adjusted to the eyecups and the hood for his jaw.

Randy Brill had broken through. As the dolphin became accustomed to working without sight and hearing, the project produced the best scientific evidence to date that a dolphin receives echolocation signals in its lower jaw. Randy had opened another window into the incredible anatomy of the most advanced acoustical animal in the world.

**Left:** At Brookfield Zoo, Nemo the dolphin helped Randy Brill achieve a breakthrough.

Many dolphins are eager to learn and be trained.

With the breakthrough also came a conclusion. It was time for Randy to say goodbye to Nemo, Shana, Stormy, and all the other dolphins at Brookfield Zoo. He traveled to a new home, in Hawaii, and to a job that would allow him to look even deeper into the unique living sonar system of the dolphin.

As a staff scientist at the Naval Ocean Systems Center Laboratory in Hawaii, Randy had a chance to work with dolphins in their own backyard—the open ocean.

The dolphins in this program learn to follow their trainers' boats to a work site. There they carry out a search-and-report mission, looking for costly equipment that might otherwise be lost under the water. If a dolphin finds something, it touches a wand at the side of the boat. The Navy started this research in the 1960s. Today it has more than one hundred dolphins in the program. Free to leave at any time, these remarkable creatures have chosen to give up their independence and stay.

# THE DOLPHIN FAMILY

More than 60 different kinds of dolphins live in the world's oceans. Some are widespread; some, extremely rare. All are members of the whale family, but scientists don't agree about exactly how they're related or how they should be classified.

These are some close relatives of the bottlenose dolphin:

• **Common dolphin:** Found worldwide in warm waters, common dolphins are often seen playing around ships and swimming with schools of tuna. They grow up to 8 feet (2.5 meters) long and are black or brown, with light strips along their sides.

• **White-sided dolphin:** A North Atlantic variety, the white-sided dolphin has bold gray, white, and yellow stripes on its side. It grows up to 9 feet (2.75 meters) long.

Pacific white-sided dolphin

• **Orca** (killer whale): The largest dolphin, the killer whale grows up to 30 feet (9 meters) long and can weigh 4 tons (3,629 kilograms). Killer whales are found worldwide and are distinctive for their bold white markings.

• **Pilot whale:** The pilot whale is the second largest type, measuring up to 20 feet (6 meters) long. Unlike other dolphins, it is all black and has a bulging rather than tapering snout.

Common dolphins

Orca

River dolphins, which also form a separate family, live in freshwater lakes and rivers in Asia and South America. They have long snouts and poor eyesight, and some are completely blind—they rely on echolocation to find fish in the murky river water. All are rare. The Chinese river dolphin is an endangered species.

Long-snouted dolphins make up a separate group. Among the most common are spinner dolphins, which often twirl on their sides when they leap out of the water, and striped and spotted dolphins.

Porpoises, which do not have the long snout characteristic of dolphins, are close relatives but are usually grouped in a separate family. They include:

• **Common or harbor porpoise:** One of the smallest dolphins, the common porpoise grows only 6 feet (2 meters) long. Common porpoises are found worldwide, but they tend to avoid people.

• **Dall's porpoise:** A Pacific Ocean variety, Dall's porpoise has bold white markings. It's a bit larger than the common porpoise and is the only porpoise that actually "porpoises"—leaps—out of the water.

Bottlenose dolphin

Scientific research suggests that exciting relationships lie ahead for humans and dolphins.

Back at Brookfield Zoo, the dolphins moved into a new home—a million-gallon tank. There, scientists like Randy Brill continue to conduct research.

Scientists and researchers have raised some exciting questions about the dolphin. They suggest that the relationship between humans and dolphins is just beginning. The work of New Explorers like Randy Brill is helping us to truly appreciate the dolphin's incredible potential.

And it's taking us ever closer to understanding why the dolphin smiles.

# GLOSSARY

**acoustic**  Having to do with sound and hearing.

**echolocation**  The ability to navigate and find objects using sound. Dolphins (and bats) send out bursts of sound. The sounds bounce off objects, and the animal's keen hearing detects the reflections.

**flukes**  The tail fins of dolphins and whales. Unlike fish tail fins, flukes are horizontal. They move up and down, not back and forth, in the water.

**humanize**  To assign human thoughts, feelings, and abilities to an animal.

**mammal**  An animal that is warm-blooded and nurses its young with milk. All mammals have backbones; most have hair or fur.

**syntax**  The way in which words are put together to form meaningful phrases.

**ultrasound imaging**  A technique in which high-frequency sound waves are used to produce an image. Ultrasound imaging is often used in medicine, to see inside the body.


# FURTHER READING

Carwardine, Mark. *Whales, Dolphins, and Porpoises.*  Boston: Houghton Mifflin, 1992.

Cousteau Society. *Dolphins.*  New York: Simon & Schuster, 1992.

Houghton, Sue. *Dolphin.*  Mahwah, NY: Troll, 1993.

Hoyt, Erich. *Riding with the Dolphins.*  Buffalo, NY: Firefly Books, 1992.

Kovacs, Deborah. *All About Dolphins.*  Seattle, WA: Third Story, 1994.

Lauder, Patricia. *Friendly Dolphins.*  New York: Scholastic, Inc., 1995.

Patent, Dorothy Hinshaw. *How Smart Are Animals?*  Orlando, FL: Harcourt Brace Javanovich, 1990.

Saunier, Nadine. *The Dolphin.*  Hauppage, NJ: Barron's, 1989.

# WEB SITES

**http://www.pbs.org/wttw/web_newexp/**
The official homepage of The New Explorers television series. Lists the show broadcast schedule, educational resources, and information about how to join The New Explorers Club as well as how to participate in The New Explorers electronic field trip.

**http://wwwa.com/dolphin/index.html**
The Wild Dolphin Project—researches and studies the habits, population and residency status of the Atlantic Dolphin in the Northern Bahamas.

**http://www.bev.net/education/SeaWorld/**
The Sea World Animal Information Database—Find out about killer whales, bottlenose dolphins, gorillas, lions, manatees, and more. Features animal information, educational resources, and career information.

**http://www.aza.org**
This homepage provides information about the many zoos and aquariums of the American Zoo and Aquarium Association, and their many conservation programs.

**http://www.nwf.org/nwf/**
The homepage of the National Wildlife Association—includes educational resources, animal and wildlife information, and a special page just for kids.

**http://www.garage.Co.jp/lilly/index.html**
The Dr. John Lilly Homepage—further information on his studies with dolphins and interspecies communication.

**http://www.cages.org/research/pepperberg/index.html**
Find out more about Dr. Irene Pepperberg and her studies in animal-human communications with Alex, the African Grey Parrot.

**http://www.dolphinresearch.org.au/**
The Dolphin Research Institute—gives school students information about dolphins: descriptions and anatomy, threats to the dolphins, protection of the dolphins, and how to help them.

**http://www.dolphin-institute.com/**
The Dolphin Institute—a research institute dedicated to dolphins and whales through education, research, and conservation; information on various studies with dolphins.

# INDEX

## Photo Credits

Page 3: Bill Arnold
Page 10: Will Crockett
All other photographic images: © Kurtis Productions Ltd. and WTTW/Chicago
Illustrations and charts: © Blackbirch Press, Inc.